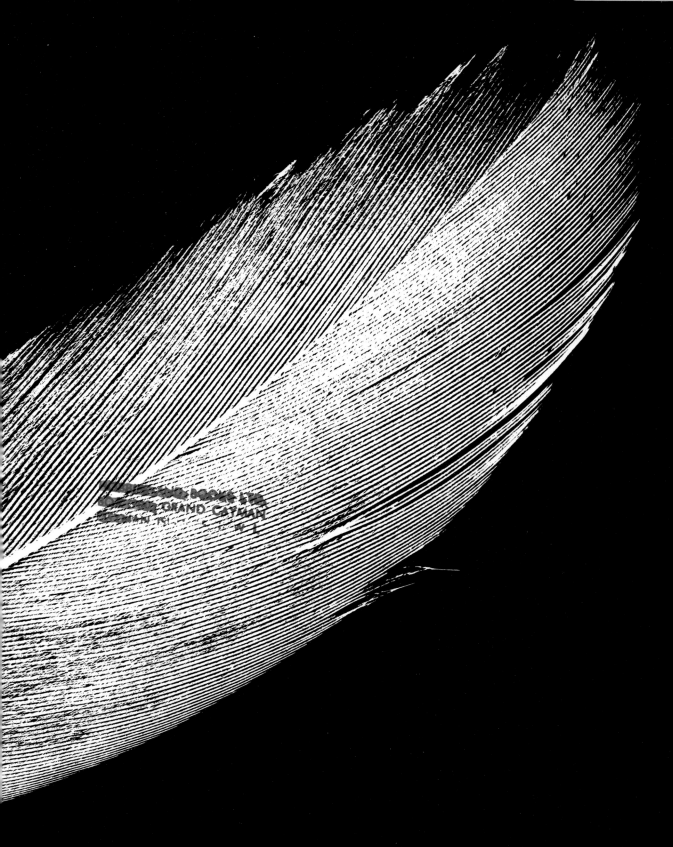

Easy Reading Edition
first published 1974
Second impression 1975

Macdonald Educational
49–50 Poland Street
London W1

Original edition
first published 1972

Adapted by Louise M Moyle
from the original text
by Dr Maurice Burton
Edited by Donald Moyle

*Illustrators*
Patricia Leander
Malcolm McGregor

*Projects*
John Taunton

*Project illustrators*
Robert Gillmor
John Yates

*Sources of Photographs*
The Zoological Society of London
The Nature Conservancy
Greenhill and Ellis

Made and printed by
Morrison and Gibb Limited
Edinburgh, Scotland

ISBN 0 356 048330

# The Life of
# Birds

# Macdonald  Educational

# The Life of Birds

This book tells you
how birds behave.

The book starts
by explaining
how birds first
began. It goes
on to show how
birds' bodies are
made, how birds
fly, how they mate
and many other things
about the way they live.

At the end of the book
are four projects
for you to do.

## Contents

# How Birds Began

The first reptiles looked like lizards. They crawled on all four legs.

Later some reptiles developed long back legs and short front legs.

These animals ran on their back legs. They started to grow feathers instead of scales.

The reptiles with feathers began to look like birds. They did not fly well.

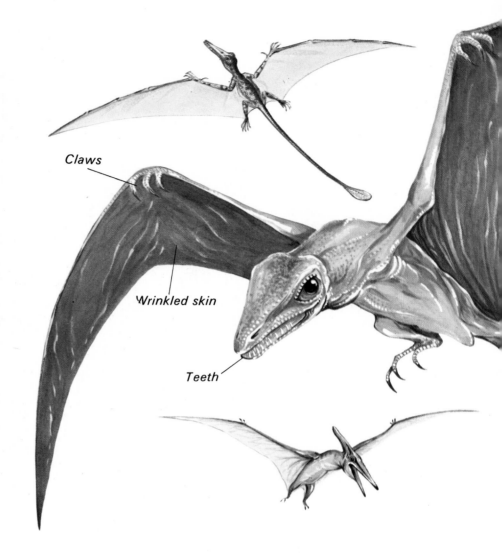

Claws

Wrinkled skin

Teeth

## The first birds

A long time ago
there were no birds. .
There were many reptiles.
A reptile is an animal
with a scaly skin
and cold blood.
Some reptiles grew
wings and feathers
and learnt to fly.

## Pterodactyls

Pterodactyls were
reptiles.

They had wings
made of skin,
but they had no feathers.
They could glide.
They were not birds.
People have found
fossils of pterodactyls.
Fossils are the remains
of animals or plants
which lived long ago.
They are found in rocks.
A fossil of one of
the first birds
has been found.

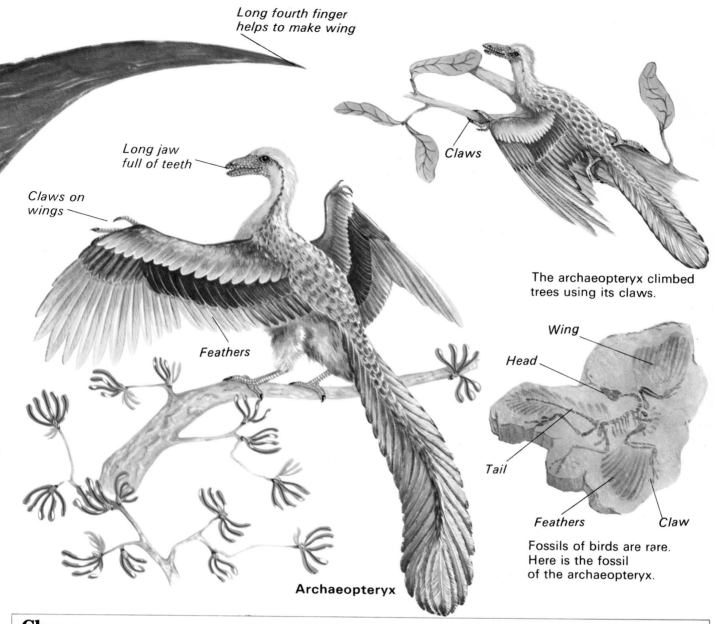

Long fourth finger
helps to make wing

Claws

The archaeopteryx climbed
trees using its claws.

Long jaw
full of teeth

Claws on
wings

Feathers

**Archaeopteryx**

Wing

Head

Tail

Feathers

Claw

Fossils of birds are rare.
Here is the fossil
of the archaeopteryx.

## Change

Changes happen
to living things
over a long time.

## Flying birds

When birds began to fly
they could escape
from enemies.
They could build nests
in trees.
These birds lived.
The others could not
fly away from enemies.

So they died out.

## Charles Darwin

A long time ago
a scientist called
Charles Darwin
went to the
Galapagos Islands.
He noticed that the
finches on each island
were different.
He realised that
animals change
to suit their surroundings.

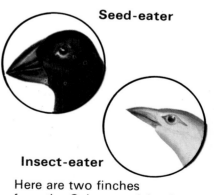

**Seed-eater**

**Insect-eater**

Here are two finches
from the Galapagos Islands.
Finches which eat seeds
have short beaks.
Finches which eat insects
have pointed beaks.

# How Birds Die Out

Hunters sometimes kill too many birds.

Cities are built on land where there used to be food and shelter for the birds.

The dodo lived on an island in the Indian Ocean. It was killed by dogs and pigs which sailors took to the island. The last dodo died 300 years ago.

**How a bird becomes extinct**

Many different kinds
of animals
have died out
since life first began.
Here are some of
the reasons for this.

**Hunting**

Many animals are killed
by people.
They are killed for food
or for sport.

If people kill too many
of one kind of animal,
that kind dies out.

**Cities**

When people build cities
they use up
the countryside.
The animals
which lived there
die out.

**Pollution**

Oil kills sea birds

by spoiling
their feathers.
Crop sprays can poison
birds and animals.

**Living safely**

Some countries have
national parks
and bird sanctuaries.
These are places
where birds
and animals
can live safely.
No one may hunt them.

The great auk lived in the North Atlantic. The last great auk was shot in 1844.

The passenger pigeon lived in North America. The last one died in a zoo in 1914.

The Labrador duck lived in North America. The last one was killed in 1875.

Moas were large birds. They lived in New Zealand. They had all been killed by 1800.

The huia lived in New Zealand. It was last seen in 1907.

The elephant bird lived in Madagascar. It died out thousands of years ago.

The Carolina parakeet was killed for its beautiful feathers and also for food.

The ivory billed woodpecker lived in North America. It was last seen in 1966.

The solitaire lived on an island in the Indian Ocean. It looked like the dodo.

# How Birds Fly

When a bird takes off, it bends its legs, spreads its wings and jumps into the air.

In the air, the bird pushes its wings down to lift itself.

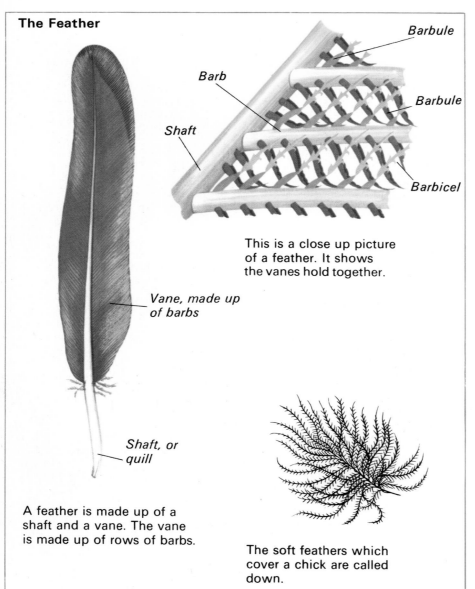

**The Feather**

*Barbule*

*Barb*

*Barbule*

*Shaft*

*Barbicel*

This is a close up picture of a feather. It shows the vanes hold together.

*Vane, made up of barbs*

*Shaft, or quill*

A feather is made up of a shaft and a vane. The vane is made up of rows of barbs.

The soft feathers which cover a chick are called down.

## Birds start to fly

The first birds
did not fly well.
Their wings were not
very strong.
Their bones were
the wrong shape.
Birds today have
more feathers
and longer wings.
They have air pockets
inside their bodies.

## In the air

When a bird moves
its wings
the wing feathers open
and close.
The feathers close
on a down beat.
They open
on an upbeat.
Some birds do not beat
their wings all the time.
They use breezes
and currents of air
to lift them up
and to move them along.
This is called gliding.

At the end of a down stroke the feathers open slightly to let air pass through. Then it begins the upstroke.

At the end of the up stroke the feathers are held together, then the bird pushes its wings down.

## Gliding and Hovering

The albatross can glide for many miles without beating its wings.

Vultures use warm air which rises into the sky. They glide with warm air.
They look out for dead animals which they can eat.

The kestrel, or windhover, stays in the sky without moving. It watches for things to eat.

Hummingbirds suck nectar from flowers. They hover in front of the flowers while they do this.

# The Senses of a Bird

**Seeing**

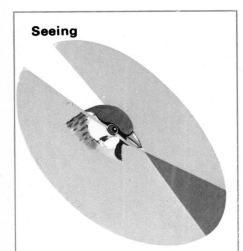

Birds need to see well to look for food and enemies. They need to see colours to find things like berries.

Birds that feed by night hunt small animals. They see things in shades of grey. They do not need to see other colours. They see straight ahead. This is best for hunting.

Owls hunt at night. They have large eyes. These help the owls to see well in the dark.

**The senses**
It is important
for a bird to see well.
But many birds
cannot smell very well.

**Looking forward**
Hawks have better
sight than people.
Their eyes are
in the front of
their heads.
They see straight
ahead.

**Looking sideways**
Small birds which
eat seeds and insects
have eyes on
the sides of their heads.
They turn their heads
to see straight ahead.

**Hearing**
The ears of a bird
are covered
with feathers.
But they can still hear
quite well.

A parrot is a day bird.
Its eyes are on the
sides of its head.

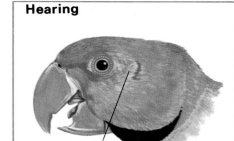

Ear

The opening of a parrot's ear
is covered with feathers.
Parrots can hear very well.

An owl can see and hear well.
It listens for mice,
and then catches them.

**Smelling**

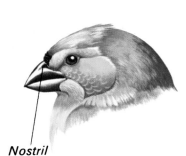

Nostril

The nostrils of most birds
are on the top of their beaks.
They are not usually used
for smelling.

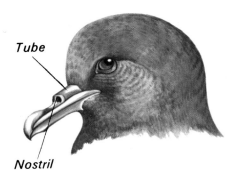

Tube

Nostril

Petrels are sea birds.
They have tubes at
the end of their noses
to help them smell
dead fishes.

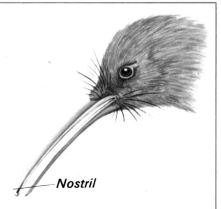

Nostril

The kiwi's nostrils
are at the tip of its beak.
It can smell worms
in the ground.

# Can Birds Think?

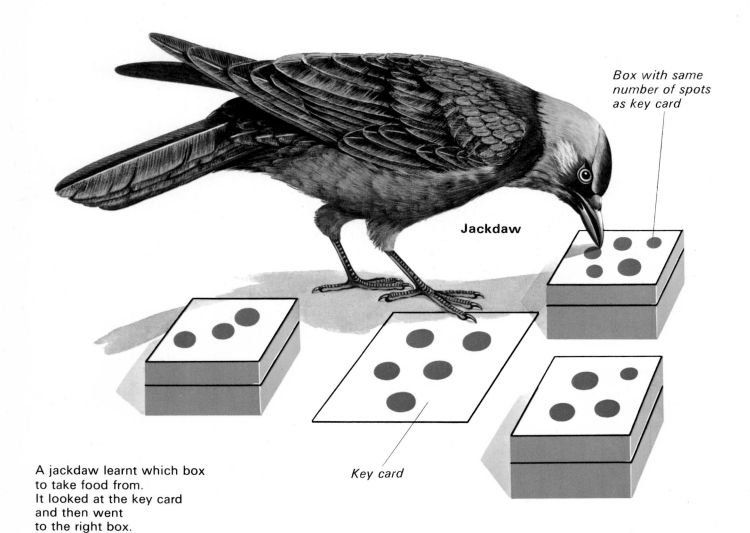

*Box with same number of spots as key card*

**Jackdaw**

*Key card*

A jackdaw learnt which box
to take food from.
It looked at the key card
and then went
to the right box.

**Instinct**
Chicks are sometimes
hatched from eggs
by keeping the eggs
in a warm box.
The chicks never see
their mother.
But they still know
how to feed themselves
and how to make nests.
Something inside
tells them what to do.
This is called instinct.
Animals do not
have to learn
the things they do
by instinct.

**Learning**
Young chicks
will peck at anything.
They soon learn which
things are good to eat,
and which are not.

**Problem solving**
Scientists made
boxes which could be
opened by pulling
a string.
They put peanuts
into each box.
Birds found that they
could pull the strings
and get the peanuts.

**Tricks**
Tame birds have time
to learn to do tricks.
Wild birds do not.
They have to
look for food instead.

## Birds Learn to Think

A gull drops a mussel on the rocks. This breaks the shell.

The woodpecker finch uses a cactus spine to pick insects out of a tree trunk.

This blue tit can pull this piece of string up and eat the peanuts fixed to it.

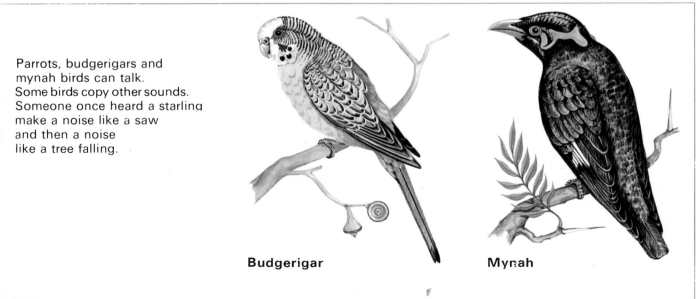

Parrots, budgerigars and mynah birds can talk. Some birds copy other sounds. Someone once heard a starling make a noise like a saw and then a noise like a tree falling.

**Budgerigar**

**Mynah**

# How a Nest is Built

*Plover pivots to make nest*

The male ringed plover turns round and round.
This makes a dip in the ground.

*The nest is in the sand*

The female lines this nest with stones and shells.

*Lining of shells*

*Eggs are hard to see*

A plover's eggs look like pebbles. They are hard to see.

*Goldfinch collects things for nest*

The hen goldfinch builds the nest by herself.

*Lining of down and wool*

Goldfinches make nests from roots, grass and moss.

*Cup-shaped nest stops eggs falling out*

A goldfinch's eggs are bluish-white with red-brown spots and streaks.

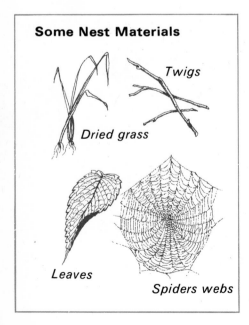

**Some Nest Materials**

*Twigs*

*Dried grass*

*Leaves*

*Spiders webs*

## Two ways to nest
Some birds make their nests on the ground.
Others build in trees or bushes.

## Building the nest
Most birds build a new nest every year.
Swallows come back to the same nest every year.
Some birds build nests in a few hours.

Other birds take days.

## Nest materials
Birds use many things to make nests.
They often use mud, dried grass and twigs.
Some birds put moss and feathers inside.
Some small birds use spiders' webs to hold their nests together.
Sea birds often use seaweed.

The male Baya weaver weaves a grass nest which looks like this.

The emperor penguin does not make a nest. It holds its egg on its feet.

The tailor bird stitches two leaves together to make a nest.

The female hornbill nests in a hollow tree. The male brings mud to the doorway of the nest. The doorway is walled up with mud.

# Finding a Mate

A male mallard does a dance
to attract the female.
He lifts his wings and tail.

Then he bobs his head
up and down.

The female mallard puts her
neck out as if she is drinking.

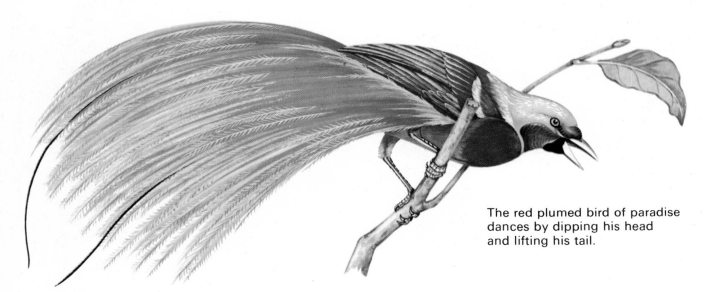

The red plumed bird of paradise
dances by dipping his head
and lifting his tail.

### Showing off
Male birds are often
more beautiful
than female birds.
Many of them
have bright colours
or very long tails.
The male bird will
show off
his bright feathers
to the female.
Some kinds of bird do
a special dance
for the female bird.

### Singing
Male birds sing
to attract
female birds.

### Gifts
Sometimes the male bird
brings his mate a gift.
He may bring food
to her, and put it
into her beak.
He may bring a stick
so they can both start
to build a nest.

### Setting up house
The birds choose
a place
to build a nest.
The male and female
usually build
the nest together.
One bird brings
things to build
the nest with.
The other bird
builds the nest.
Sometimes one bird
does all the work.

A peacock has long tail feathers.

He spreads them out to make a fan.

He struts about so that the peahen notices him.

The crestless gardener makes a hut of sticks around a small tree. He puts flowers there.

# The Birth of a Bird

Male and female birds mate before the hen lays an egg. When mating the male bird gets on to the female's back. He sends a fluid full of sperm from his body into the body of the female. This reaches the egg cells in her ovaries. Sperm goes into the egg cell. This is how a chick begins. The egg is then laid.

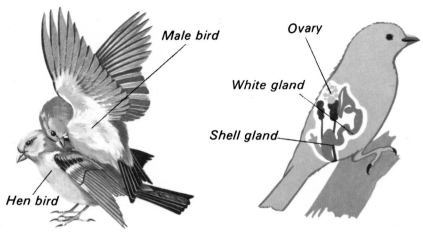

*Male bird*

*Hen bird*

*Ovary*

*White gland*

*Shell gland*

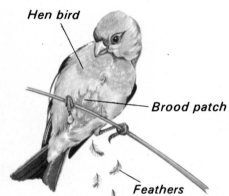
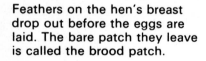

*Hen bird*

*Brood patch*

*Feathers*

Feathers on the hen's breast drop out before the eggs are laid. The bare patch they leave is called the brood patch.

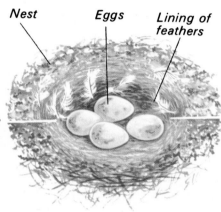

*Nest*  *Eggs*  *Lining of feathers*

Many birds line their nests with feathers. These make a warm lining for the eggs when they are laid.

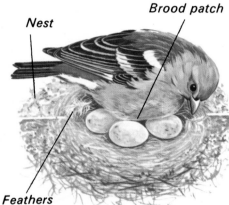

*Nest*  *Brood patch*

*Feathers*

The hen sits on the eggs. She keeps the eggs warm with her brood patch.

Inside an egg you see the white and the yolk. The yolk is the food for the chick. The chick starts as a spot in the yolk. Air gets through the shell to the chick.

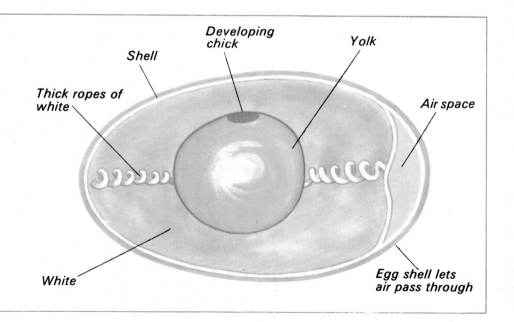

*Shell*  *Developing chick*  *Yolk*

*Thick ropes of white*

*Air space*

*White*

*Egg shell lets air pass through*

## Breeding

Birds mate
at a special time
of the year.
A male and a female
bird form a pair.
They mate.
After this the female
lays her eggs.
The chicks grow
inside the eggs.
Each chick starts
as an egg cell.
This cell grows
into a chick
if it joins with
a sperm cell.
The sperm cell comes
from a male bird.
The egg cell splits up
again and again.
It becomes many cells.
These cells make
the body of the
chick.

## Laying the eggs

Some birds
take one minute
to lay an egg.
A cuckoo takes
a few seconds.
A turkey can take
two hours.

## When are eggs laid?

Some birds lay eggs
at special times
of day.
They lay
one egg at a time.
The next egg is laid
the next day, or later.

Eggs must be kept warm
so that the chick can grow.

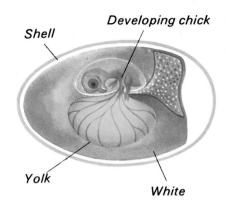

Shell

Developing chick

Yolk

White

The chick uses the yolk
as food. The white dries up.

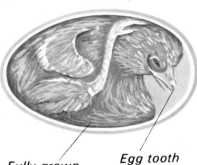

Fully grown
chick

Egg tooth

The chick grows as big as
the shell. It has a tooth
on the end of its beak.

The chick taps on the shell
with the tooth. The chick
pushes with its head.

The shell is broken.
The tooth drops off.
The chick is wet and tired.

The chick dries out.
It soon begins to peck for food.

# Why are Eggs Different?

**Owl's egg**

**Owl**

Owls nest in
dark, hollow trees. The eggs
are white and round.

**Plover's egg**

**Plover**

Plovers nest in
sandy ground.
The eggs
are the colour of the ground.

**Guillemot's egg**

**Guillemot**

A guillemot's eggs are laid on
a cliff. They are pear
shaped. They roll in a circle.
They cannot fall off the cliff.

**Owl's nest**

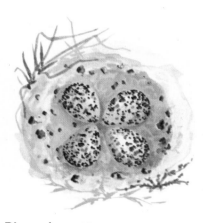

**Plover's nest**

**Guillemot's nest**

**Why eggs?**
If birds carried
their babies
inside them,
they would find
it hard to fly far.
They lay eggs instead.

**Kinds of eggs**
There are more
than 8000 different
kinds of birds.
Their eggs are all
different sizes
and colours.
Birds which lay
large eggs
often lay only a few.
Birds which lay
small eggs
often lay several.

**Shapes of eggs**
Most birds' eggs
have a blunt end
and a pointed end.
Eggs this shape
will not roll very far
out of the nest.
Eggs laid in hollows
will not roll out.
They are round.

**Colours**
Some eggs are
coloured and have
spots or lines.
This makes it hard
for enemies
to see the eggs.
Eggs laid in dark
places are white.

**Sizes of Eggs**

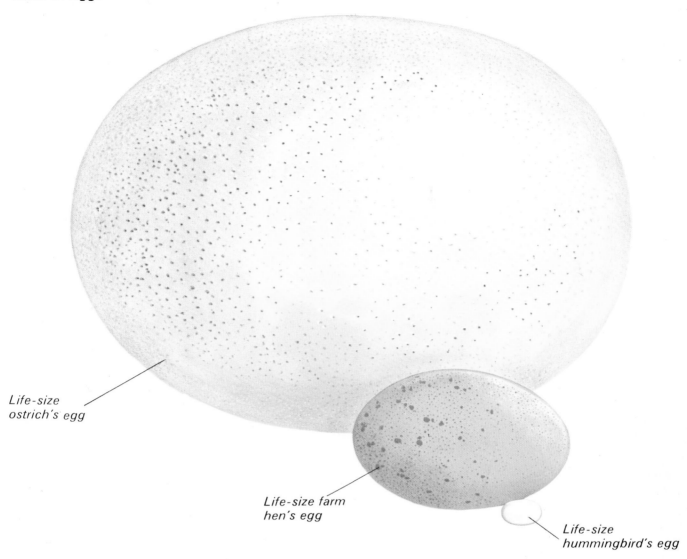

*Life-size
ostrich's egg*

*Life-size farm
hen's egg*

*Life-size
hummingbird's egg*

**Did You Know?**

*Cuckoo's egg*

*Square 'egg'*

*Real egg*

If a pheasant's eggs are stolen
she will go on and lay some more.

Black headed gulls like
square shaped
models of their eggs
better than their own eggs,
if the models are bigger.

Cuckoos lay their eggs
in other birds' nests.
Here is a cuckoo's egg
in the nest of a meadow pipit.

# Growing Up

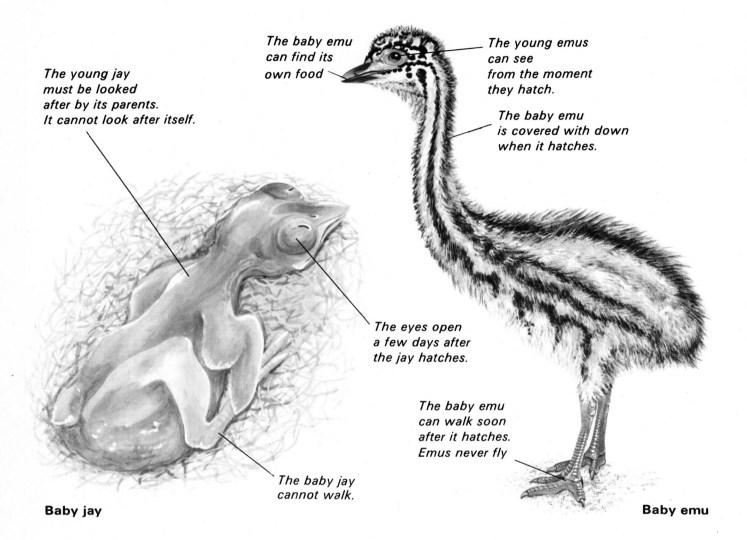

The young jay must be looked after by its parents. It cannot look after itself.

The baby emu can find its own food

The young emus can see from the moment they hatch.

The baby emu is covered with down when it hatches.

The eyes open a few days after the jay hatches.

The baby emu can walk soon after it hatches. Emus never fly

The baby jay cannot walk.

**Baby jay**

**Baby emu**

Nest in tree

Nest on ground

A nest on the ground is not safe. A cat could find the nest and kill the baby birds.

### Nests on the ground

Some birds build nests on the ground. Baby birds hatched in these nests can soon run about and find food. The babies have down which is the colour of the place where they live. If they are afraid, they stand very still This makes it hard for enemies to see them.

### Nests off the ground

Some birds have nests in trees. Baby birds hatched in trees are looked after by their parents. They have to be fed. They have to learn to fly, and to look after themselves.

Baby birds hatched
in trees do not
have feathers.
They cannot see.

Baby birds hatched on the
ground run about
as soon as they are hatched.

Baby birds hatched in trees
soon grow feathers.
Then they leave the nest.

At first, baby magpies
have no feathers.

The young magpie
has a short tail.

Here is a fully grown magpie.
It has a very long tail.

# How Birds Eat

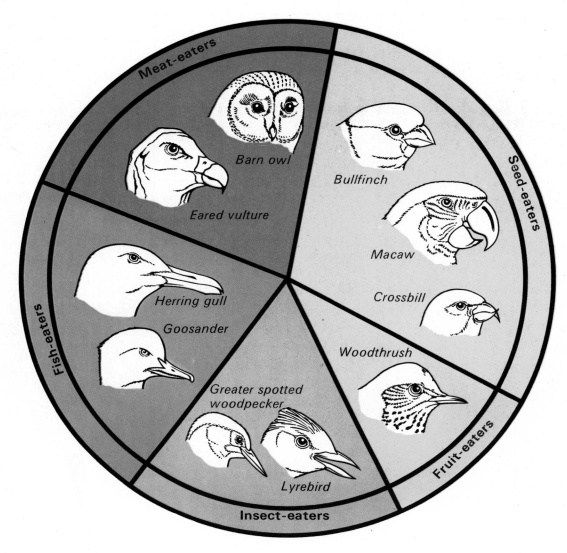

Meat-eaters

Barn owl

Eared vulture

Seed-eaters

Bullfinch

Macaw

Crossbill

Woodthrush

Fish-eaters

Herring gull

Goosander

Greater spotted woodpecker

Lyrebird

Insect-eaters

Fruit-eaters

**Beaks**
The shape of a
bird's beak
is made to suit
the food it eats.

**Seed eaters**
Finches have short
beaks.
They use their beaks
to crack the shells
of seeds.
Crossbills pick seeds
out of pine cones.

Seed-eaters need
to have strong beaks.

**Fruit eaters**
Some birds eat fruit.
They have long beaks.
These do not need
to be very strong.

**Insect eaters**
The lyre bird has
a long thin beak.
It picks up insects
from the ground.

Woodpeckers have
long, strong beaks.
They eat insects
out of tree trunks.

**Fish eaters**
Kingfishers
and herons
have beaks
shaped like daggers.
They use these
sharp beaks
to catch fishes.
Gulls have

A kiwi has a long beak.
It pushes its beak into the
ground to find earthworms.
The kiwi has nostrils
on the end of its beak.
It can smell the earthworms.

The oxpecker lives in Africa.
It eats ticks. Ticks live
on the backs of animals
like the hippopotamus.
The oxpecker runs
on the backs of animals
and eats the ticks.

hooked beaks
for holding fishes.
The goosander duck
has a beak
with horny edges.
This helps the bird
to hold on to fishes.

## Meat eaters

Owls, hawks
and vultures
all eat meat.
They have hooked beaks
for tearing meat.

Gulls eat mussels. They drop
the mussels on to rocks
to break the shells.

The Egyptian vulture eats
ostrich eggs. The vulture
drops a stone on to
the egg to break the shell.

# Inside a Bird

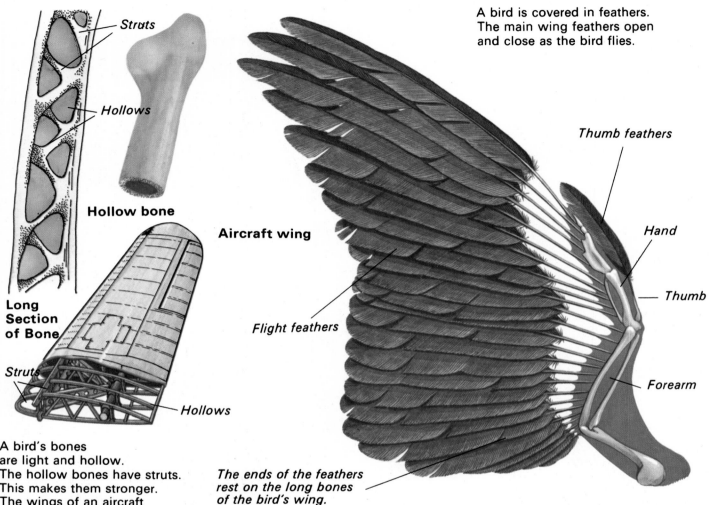

Struts

Hollows

**Hollow bone**

**Aircraft wing**

**Long
Section
of Bone**

Struts

Hollows

A bird's bones
are light and hollow.
The hollow bones have struts.
This makes them stronger.
The wings of an aircraft
are built in the same way.

A bird is covered in feathers.
The main wing feathers open
and close as the bird flies.

*Thumb feathers*

*Hand*

*Thumb*

*Flight feathers*

*Forearm*

*The ends of the feathers
rest on the long bones
of the bird's wing.*

Lung

Lung

Air sacs

Air sacs

The lungs of a bird
lead into air sacs.
These sacs hold extra air.

## Flying

A bird's body
is made to fly.
The bones are light
and hollow.
Birds have strong
muscles.

## Keeping warm

Birds often have
soft down feathers
under their other
feathers.
These help to keep

the birds warm.

## Keeping cool

Birds can get hot
when they are
flying fast.
Birds take air
into their lungs.
This air goes into
air sacs.
When the birds
breathe out
the heat
leaves their bodies.

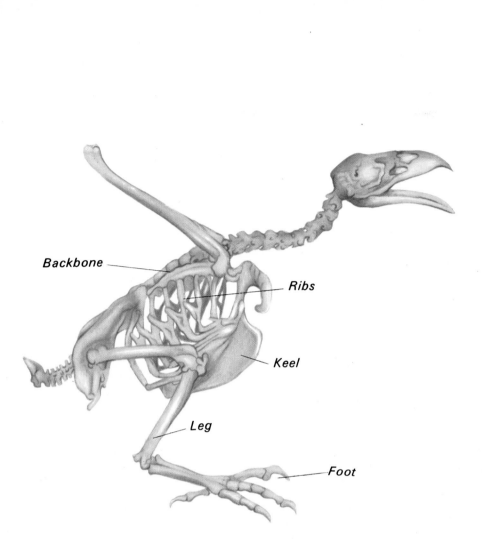

Backbone

Ribs

Keel

Leg

Foot

This is a bird's skeleton.
The bird has long wing bones,
and long leg bones.

The muscle on each side of
the breast bone is strong.
It moves the wings
as the bird flies.

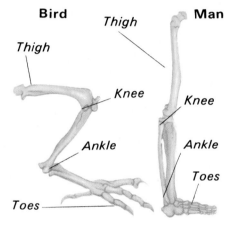

**Bird**  **Man**

Thigh

Thigh

Knee

Knee

Ankle

Ankle

Toes

Toes

Here are the bones
of a bird's leg and
a man's leg.
They are very different.

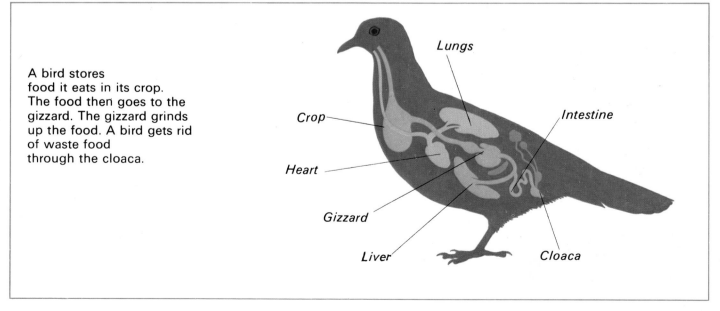

A bird stores
food it eats in its crop.
The food then goes to the
gizzard. The gizzard grinds
up the food. A bird gets rid
of waste food
through the cloaca.

Lungs

Crop

Intestine

Heart

Gizzard

Liver

Cloaca

# Private Property

Sea birds only need
a small piece of land for
their territory. They catch
their food in the sea.

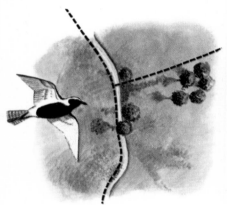

A plover chooses
a part of a field
for his territory.
The lines show the border.

Swallows do not need
any territory. They catch and
eat insects in the air.

A golden eagle needs three
miles of land to hunt in.

## Territory

Some birds stay
in flocks in winter.
When spring comes
the flock breaks up.
Each male bird
chooses a place
in a tree.
He sings in places
around the tree.
These places
are called song posts.
The bird is telling
other birds that
this is his territory.

## Pairs of birds

A female bird
hears the male sing.
She flies
to his branch.
If she likes the male
she stays on the branch.
The two birds
look for food
in their territory.
They keep other birds
away from it.

# Quarrelling Birds

These wagtails are quarrelling about territory.

Falcons have large claws. They use these to protect themselves.

The cassowary has a long claw on each foot. This claw can kill a man.

Skuas are sea birds. They will attack a man who comes near their nests.

## Defence

Birds do not
often fight.
They would rather
fly away.
Some large birds
will fight
if they have to.
Hawks and eagles
use their claws
for defence.
Herons use
their strong beaks
as daggers.

## Quarrelling

Birds sometimes quarrel.
But they do not
hurt each other much.
A male bird will fluff
out his feathers
if another bird
comes on to
his territory.
He does this to
make himself
look fierce.
The other bird
will fly off.

# Bird Language

## Making Sounds

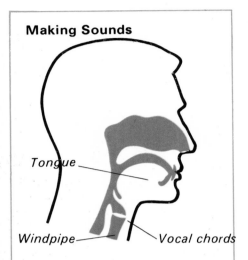

*Tongue*

*Windpipe* — *Vocal chords*

Air goes past the vocal chords when we speak. The vocal chords vibrate. This makes a sound.

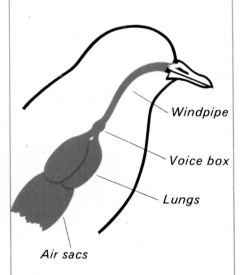

*Windpipe*

*Voice box*

*Lungs*

*Air sacs*

A bird does not have vocal chords. It has a voice box which has a lot of small muscles. These change the shape of the voice box. So the bird can make many different sounds.

The nightingale sings both at night and in the day. It has a beautiful song.

## Bird song

Birds make many sounds. A bird sings to warn other birds to keep off his territory. A bird will also sing to attract a mate.

## Size and sound

Some small birds can sing very loudly.

Some large birds make very little noise.

## Bird calls

Birds often make sounds known as calls. This is not the same as singing. Birds call when danger is near. Some birds call to tell other birds they have found food.

## Call to Food

Gulls call when they find food. They call if they see a lot of fishes. Other gulls hear the calls and come to share the fishes.

## Love Call

Birds sing to their mates. Some birds make other sounds to their mates. A woodpecker drums on a tree trunk with his beak.

## Call for Help

Glass cage

Wall

Chick calling for help

Mother hen

Chick calling for help

A hen makes a clucking sound. The chicks make a cheeping sound. The chicks can find their mother when she clucks. The hen can find her chicks when she hears them cheep. She cannot hear the chick in the glass dome. So she will not come and help it.

35

# Colours of Birds

**Blue-crowned pigeon**

**Scarlet macaw**

## Using colour

Birds can recognise
each other
from their colours.
Dull colours help
to make a bird
hard to see.
Some birds are
brightly coloured.
This helps
to attract a mate.

## Different colours

Birds which live
in snowy lands
are white.
Birds which come out
at night often
have dull colours.
Birds in hot
countries often have
bright colours.
They cannot easily
be seen among
the flowers and trees.
The two birds
in the pictures
live in hot countries.

Snowy owls live in the Arctic.
Their winter feathers
do not show up
against the snow.

A penguin's black back
does not show up in the sea.
Enemies swimming
underneath the penguin
cannot easily see its white front.

The robin has a red breast.
He shows his red breast
to warn other robins
not to come into his territory.

A buzzard has marks
under its wings, like
the marks on the
wings of a warplane.

Sand grouse chicks are
a sandy colour.
They are hard to see.

The male frigate bird
shows off to the female
by blowing up a red bag
he has under his chin.

# Migration

### The Seasons

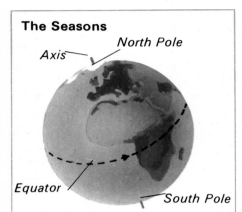

The earth is round.
It is also
slightly tilted.
It moves round the sun.
It takes the earth $365\frac{1}{4}$ days
to move round the sun.

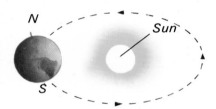

When the south
is near the sun,
it is summer in the south.

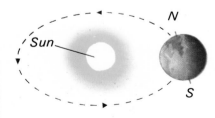

When the north
is near the sun,
it is summer in the north.

Swallows meet together
when it is time to migrate.

### Migration

Birds often fly
from one country
to another.
This is called
migration.
Birds migrate
to places where
they can find food.

### Swallows

Swallows live
in South Africa.
When winter comes
in South Africa
they fly north
to Europe.
There is food there,
because it is summer.
The swallows fly
back to South Africa
at the end of
the summer.
They do this every year.
Swallows know
that winter is coming
when the days
get shorter.

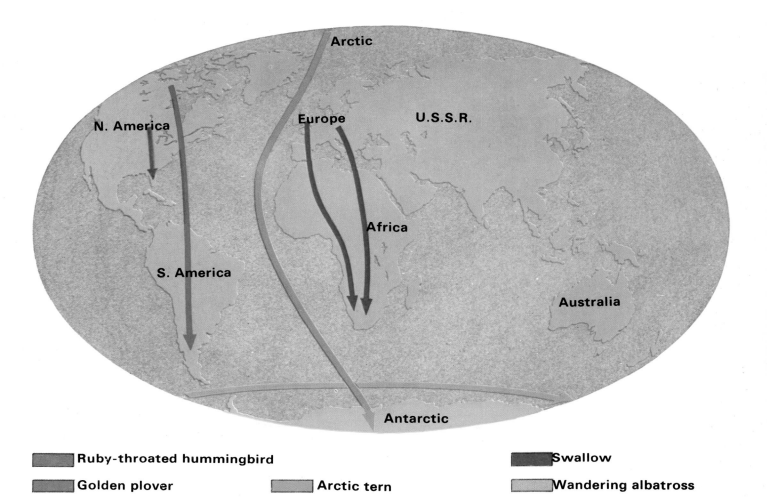

**Ruby-throated hummingbird**

**Golden plover**

**Arctic tern**

**Swallow**

**Wandering albatross**

This map shows the ways different birds migrate.

The arrows show where the different birds fly.

You can see that some birds migrate further than others.

Birds often migrate in flocks.

These geese are migrating.

They fly in a V-shape like this.

# Finding the Way

**American robin**

**Blue jay**

Some birds migrate by day.
They use the sun
to help them find their way.

These birds are in a cage.
They are ready to migrate.
They face the sun when it shines.

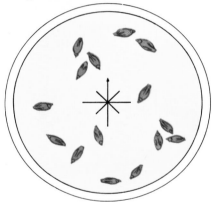

If it is cloudy, the birds
cannot see the sun.
They do not know which way
to face.

### Which way?
Birds use
the sun, the stars
and the moon to help
to find their way.
They can get lost.
if it is cloudy.

### Cuckoos
Mother cuckoos
lay their eggs
in other birds' nests.
They leave them there.
The parent birds fly
to Africa
for the winter.
The young cuckoo
finds its own way
a month later.

### Travelling
Birds fly at about
4,000 feet (1,200 m)
above the ground.
They have a rest
after 50 miles (80 km).
During one day they can
travel 500 miles (800 km).

Pigeons can be trained
to fly home if they
are taken a long way away.
Because of this, people often
use pigeons to carry messages.

**Rose breasted grosbeak**

**Great-crested fly catcher**

Many birds migrate at night.
They use the stars and moon
to help them find their way.

These birds are in a dome
with a picture of the night sky.
The birds think the picture
is the real sky.
They face the way they
will have to migrate.

If it is foggy, the birds
lose their way. Sometimes
they crash into lighthouses

These migrating birds can be
seen against the moon.

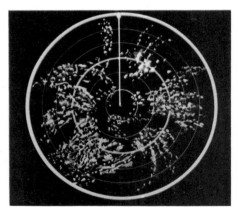

Migrating birds can be seen
on a radar screen.

People put rings on
some birds.
If anyone catches the bird
later, they can see where
the bird has migrated from.

# Birds in Groups

Nest made of palm fronds

Village weaver birds live in Africa. They make a lot of nests in one palm tree.

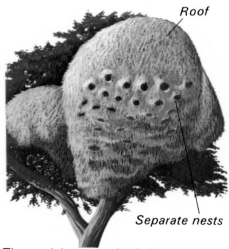

Roof

Separate nests

The social weaver birds live in Africa. There are many nests under one roof.

## Company
Some birds live on their own. They only meet other birds in the breeding season. Most birds like company. Some live in large flocks or in pairs.

## Helping each other
Birds which live in groups can help each other. They can all look for food. They can warn each other when enemies come near.

## Colonies
Some flocks of birds all build nests close to each other. Each pair of birds builds its own nest. This is called a breeding colony.

Penguins like to live close together.
This helps them to keep
each other warm.

Starlings stay in flocks.
They fly very close
together if a hawk comes near.

*Hawk*

*Flock
of starlings*

Flamingos live in big groups.    They fly around together.    They nest together.

# Strange Behaviour

## The Pecking Order

A

B

C

A is the boss hen.
She may peck the other hens.
They do not peck her.
B is the second hen.
She may peck all the hens
except A. C is the third hen.
She may peck all the hens
except A and B.
There are many more hens.

## Strutting

Some birds do things
which look odd.
They may strut around.
Male birds do this
to attract
female birds.
They may be trying
to tell other birds
to keep away
from their territory.

## Puzzles

Some birds rub ants
on to their wing feathers.
Blue tits sometimes
peck at the putty
round a window.
They may come indoors
and peck the wallpaper
or at books.
No one knows why
birds do these things.

Pecking birds sometimes
pick up ants in their beaks.
They rub the ants
under their wing feathers.
The acid from the ants
may be good for the feathers.

If an enemy comes near,
a lapwing runs from her nest.
She pretends she has
a broken wing.
The enemy chases her
and leaves the nest alone.

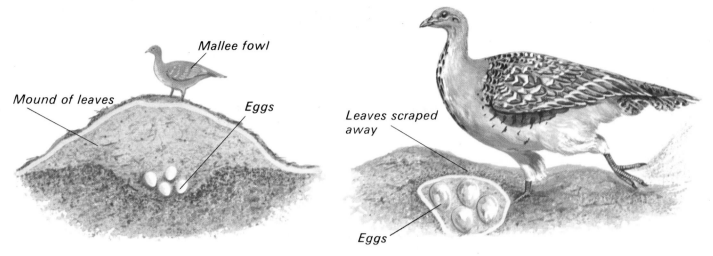

A mallee fowl lays ner eggs in a pile of dry leaves.

If the nest gets hot, the cock bird opens the pile.

When the nest is cool, he covers up the pile of leaves.

Swifts sometimes sleep when they are in the air.

Jays bury acorns and can find them in the winter.

A poorwill bird was once found hibernating.
Birds do not often do this.

Magpies steal shiny things.
They like to hide them.
No one knows why.

# How Birds Die

The peregrine falcon swoops down from the sky to attack other birds.

Peregrine falcon

Pheasant

Some birds cannot see straight ahead. They bump into things.

Cats often catch and kill young birds.

Some young birds fall to the ground when they are learning to fly.

## Young birds

Some birds die young.
Crows and rats can
kill young birds.
Some birds get sick.
Some birds fall
when they
are learning to fly.
Others die because
they get too cold.
Three young birds
out of every five
die before
they are six months old.

## Where do sick birds go?

We do not often
see dead birds.
Sick birds find holes
to creep into before
they die.

## Cold weather

Birds may starve
in cold weather.
They may not be able
to find food
in icy ground.
They cannot find water.

# Pollution

Many seabirds die like this one.　　It is covered with oil.　　The oil has come from ships.

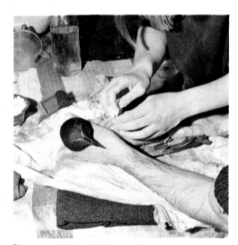

Some of the birds can be cleaned. After that they are set free. They can look after themselves again.

## Oil
Some things
which people use
can harm birds.
Oil from ships
is sometimes
spilled into the sea.
The oil sticks to the
birds' feathers.
The birds cannot fly
or swim properly.
They cannot
catch food
and so they starve.

## Chemicals
Weed killer
and insect killer
can harm birds.
Birds may eat
poisoned insects.
These harm birds.
Ospreys eat fish
which have eaten
poisoned insects.
After that, the osprey
may not lay any eggs.
If it does lay eggs,
these may not hatch.

# Stories about Birds

Phoenix

Dove

Stork

Pelican

Geese

## The Phoenix

The Phoenix
does not really
exist. Stories say
it builds a nest, then
it sets itself on fire.
Three days later
it grows up again
from the ashes.

## Symbols and stories

The white dove is
a symbol of peace.
But doves are not
very peaceful birds.
They often quarrel.
The pelican is
a symbol of piety.
Storks are symbols
of good luck.
There is also a story
that storks bring
new babies.
Once some invaders
tried to capture Rome.
But the geese in Rome
made a noise
and woke the people.

# Facts and Figures

**Largest land bird**
The ostrich is up to
9 feet (2.7 m) tall.
It weighs up to
345 lb (156 kg).

**Heaviest flying bird**
The mute swan
weighs up to $50\frac{1}{2}$ lb (23 kg).

**Smallest flying bird**
The bee humming bird
is $2\frac{1}{4}$ inches (57 mm) long
and only weighs $\frac{1}{16}$ oz (1.8 g).

**Greatest wing span**
The marabou stork
has a wing span of
12 feet (3.7 m).

**Longest migration**
The arctic tern
flies 22,000 miles (34,400 km)
from the Antarctic to
the Arctic and back.

**Fastest speed in the air**
The spine tailed swift
flies over 100 m.p.h. (161 km/h)
when it is flying along.
The peregrine falcon
can dive at 180 m.p.h.
(290 km/h) when it is
catching its prey.

**Fastest speed on the land**
The ostrich can reach
37 m.p.h. (60 km/h).

**Fastest speed under water**
The gentoo penguin
can reach a speed of
22 m.p.h. (35 km/h).

**Greatest height flown**
The Egyptian goose
can fly 35,000 feet up
in the air.

**Fastest wing beats**
The humming bird
beats its wings at 200
beats a second when it
is hovering.

**Greatest number of wing beats**
When the golden plover
migrates it makes
two wing beats every
second. It flies for
35 hours. This means
it makes 252,000
wing beats.

**Greatest depth reached by a diving bird**
A loon can dive
240 feet (73 m).

**Longest stay under water**
The Adelie penguin
can stay under water for
three minutes. It may
be able to stay under water
for five minutes.

**Largest egg**
An ostrich's
egg is eight
inches (203 mm) long.
It weighs more than
31 lb (14 kg).

**Smallest egg**
The bee humming bird's
egg is $\frac{3}{16}$ inch
(4.5 mm) long. It only
weighs $\frac{5}{1000}$ oz (0.14 g).

**Largest clutch of eggs**
A mallard duck
can lay up to 16 eggs.
The mallard will lay
up to a hundred eggs
if someone takes them
away as soon as the
duck lays them. Farm hens
can lay one egg almost
every day of the year.

They lay fewer eggs
as they get older.

**Longest nesting season**
The mallee fowl's
nesting season lasts
eleven months.

**Commonest bird**
The starling
is found in most parts
of the world.

**Rarest bird**
The noisy scrub bird
of Australia is very rare.
Everyone thought it
had died out. Then it was
found again in 1961.

**Longest lived bird**
An eagle owl has been known
to live 68 years.
It was a tame
one, living safely.
A wild herring gull
once lived for 32 years.
Some people say
cockatoos can live for
nearly 100 years.

**Longest time airborne**
Swifts spend most
of their time in the air.
They can even sleep there.

**Biggest pest**
The dioch of Africa
eats grain.
Sometimes, so many
diochs land on a tree
that they break the branches.
They will make about
6,000 nests in one
big tree. There could
be 200 million nests in
5,000 acres (2,000 ha).

**Kinds of birds**
There are more than

8,000 different kinds
of bird.
There were 8,580 kinds
in 1962.

## Nests
Some kinds of penguin
make no nest.
They keep their eggs warm
on their feet.
Cuckoos do not make a nest.
They lay their eggs
in the nests of other birds.
The long tailed tit
makes a very complicated
nest. It holds two
parent birds, and about
twelve babies. The nest
is made of moss, cobwebs,
hair and lichens.
Tits line their nests
with feathers.
Pigeons build
very rough nests.
Crows can make nests
on telegraph wires.
A blackbird once stole lace
and used it in a nest.
Wrens live close together
when it is cold.
Once, 52 were found in
a nest box.
Storks make nests on top of
houses.
The smallest nest is made
by the humming bird.
It is only $\frac{4}{5}$ inch (20 mm)
across and one inch
(25 mm) high.

## Feeding
Tits feed their young on
caterpillars.
Tits can collect
over 10,000 caterpillars
while they are feeding
their young.

## Time taken for eggs to hatch
Small bird's eggs take two
weeks. A wandering albatross'
egg takes 73 days.
A kiwi's egg takes 80 days.

## Time taken for baby birds to grow proper feathers.
Baby birds are covered
with down when they
hatch out. They shed
their down and
grow feathers.
Most small birds
take 2 weeks to do this.
Pigeons, nightjars,
hummingbirds and woodpeckers
take four weeks.
The smaller albatross
takes 20-21 weeks.
The emperor penguin
takes 35-39 weeks.
The wandering albatross
takes 44-45 weeks.

## Why some kinds of birds are dying out
Many kinds of birds
are dying out.
If there are only
a few of one kind left,
it is easy for them all
to be killed. They may
be killed in a typhoon,
or in a cold winter.
Birds die out
for many reasons.
People cut down the forests
where they live.
There is nowhere for
the birds to live.
Some kinds of bird
are hunted until
there are none left alive.

## Dying out
These birds are all
in danger of dying out:

## Californian condor
This is a kind
of vulture. Condors
have lived in America
for 10,000 years.
They lived all over
America.
People have shot them.
Now there may
only be 50 left.

## Everglade kite
These birds are dying
out because people
have disturbed them
while the birds are
nesting.
Other birds steal their eggs.
There are only about
12 everglade kites left now.

## Galapagos hawk
These are really
a kind of buzzard.
They live on the Galapagos islands
in the Pacific Ocean.
People shoot the hawks
because they eat chickens.
Goats have eaten
a lot of the food
which the hawks need.
Now there are only
about 200 left.

## Monkey-eating eagle
This bird comes
from the Philippines.
People there like to have
stuffed eagles in
their houses.
The eagles are often killed.
Now there are
only a hundred left.

## Whooping crane
This bird lives
in Canada. It goes
to Texas for the winter.
People have shot
many of these birds.
Now there are only
about 50 left.

## Eskimo curlew
There used to be
many of these birds.
They nested in the Arctic.
Every year
they flew to South America.
They flew back
to the Arctic each spring.
People shot them as they flew.
Only a few birds
reached the Arctic.

No one has seen
the nests of these birds
for 30 years.

**New Zealand laughing owl**
This owl used to live
all over New Zealand.
It also lived in other parts of
the South Pacific.
The last one was seen
in 1914. People know
there are still some left
as they have heard
their call.

**Ivory-billed woodpecker**
This is a big woodpecker.
It has black, white
and red feathers.
A pair of these woodpeckers
needs 2,000 acres (800 ha)
of forest to live in.
They eat the grubs of insects
which live in dead trees.
The woodpeckers lived
in the forests of
North America and Cuba.
People have cut down
many trees in these forests.
Everyone thought that
the ivory billed woodpecker
had died out.
But some were seen
a few years ago.
Some forest trees
have been left for
the woodpeckers.

**Takahe**
People in the 19th century
found the bones of this bird.
They thought the bird
had died out.
Later, some skins
and dead birds were found.
There was an expedition in 1949
to look for takahes.
They were found high up
in the mountains
in the South Island
of New Zealand.
There were about 200
or 300 birds there.
The place where they were found
is a nature reserve now.

**Noisy scrub bird**
This is a very noisy bird.
It lived in scrub land
in Western Australia.
People cleared the scrub
away.
The birds had nowhere
to live.
Everyone thought
that scrub birds had died out.
Then someone saw one
in 1961.
A nature reserve
was set up in that place.
There are about 100
noisy scrub birds
living there now.

# Glossary

**Bird**
A bird is a warm blooded
animal whose body
is covered in feathers.

**Flying**
A bird is flying when it is
moving through the air
by beating its wings.

**Gliding**
A bird is gliding when it
moves through the air
without flapping its wings.

**Hovering**
A bird is hovering
when it stays in place
in the air and makes
only small wing beats.

**Plumage**
All the feathers
on a bird's body.

**Train**
The extra long tail
of peacocks and pheasants.

**Down**
The small soft feathers
on a baby bird.
Many birds have
an undercoat of down
all their lives.

**To gape**
To open the beak wide,
showing the throat.

**Crop**
A thin bag of skin
opening into the gullet.
The bird stores food there.

**Gizzard**
The bird's stomach.

**Air sacs**
Bags of skin
leading from the lungs
into the bird's body.

**Breeding season**
The time of the year when
birds mate.

**Incubating**
Keeping the eggs warm
so that they hatch.

**To hatch**
To break out of the egg.

**Brood**
The baby birds hatched from
the clutch of eggs.

**Brood patch**
A bald patch
on the breast of a bird.
It comes when eggs
have to be kept warm.

**Clutch**
A complete set of eggs
laid by one female.

**Fledgling**
A young bird with its
first set of grown up feathers.

**Migration**
When birds go
from one feeding place
to a breeding place
a long way away.

**Evolution**
Living things change
over thousands of years.
This change is called
evolution.

# How to Watch Birds

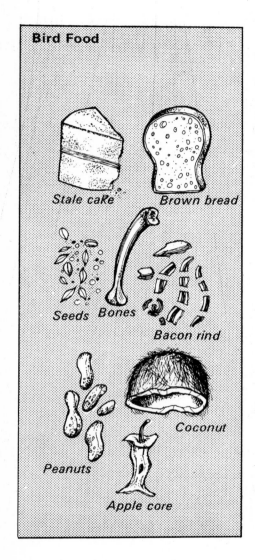

**Bird Food**

Stale cake

Brown bread

Seeds  Bones

Bacon rind

Peanuts

Coconut

Apple core

### Looking at birds
It is interesting to
watch birds.
You can watch them
from your own home.
Birds will come into
your garden if you put
out food and water.

### Food
Put food on the ground,
or on a bird table.
Put water in a dish.

### Which bird?
Try to learn the names
of the birds you see.

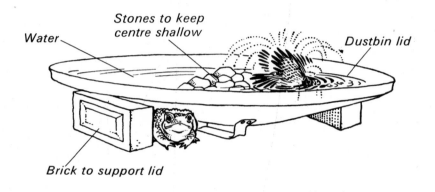

Water

Stones to keep
centre shallow

Dustbin lid

Brick to support lid

Make a bird bath
from an old dustbin lid.
Support the lid
with bricks and stones.

Watch the birds come
to bathe.

House sparrow

Wren

Dunnock

Chaffinch

Robin

Always look at a bird's beak.
You can see what
food the bird eats. Birds
with short beaks eat seeds.
A pointed beak shows
that a bird eats insects.
This will help you
to find out
the names of the birds.

## What to look for

Draw a picture of the bird you see. Show the shape of its beak, and show where the different colours are. Now you can find the bird's name by looking it up in a book.

## Books

These books will help you: *The Observers Book of Birds* (published by Warne) and *The Field Guide to the Birds of Britain and Europe* (published by Collins).

## What you need

Binoculars will help you to see birds without being very close to them. Use a large scale map to work out where to find the best places for bird-watching. A map will also help you to get there.

## Hiding

Try to hide when you are watching birds. Hide in a hedge, or make a screen of branches. You could hide in a tent.

## Habitats

The place where a bird lives is called its habitat. Make a note of the different kinds of habitat where birds live. Some birds are seen in woods. Others are seen on farm land or by the sea. Soon, you will learn which birds to expect in different places.

If you look through binoculars, the bird will look bigger.

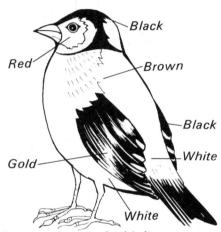

Draw a picture of a bird. Find out from a book which bird it is.

| Date | Time | Name of Bird | Food Eaten | Drink | Bathe |
|------|------|-------------|-----------|-------|-------|
|      |      |             |           |       |       |

Keep a list of the birds you see.

Write down the date, the time, and the name of the bird you saw.

Write down the food they eat, and whether they drink or bathe.

# Making a Nest Box

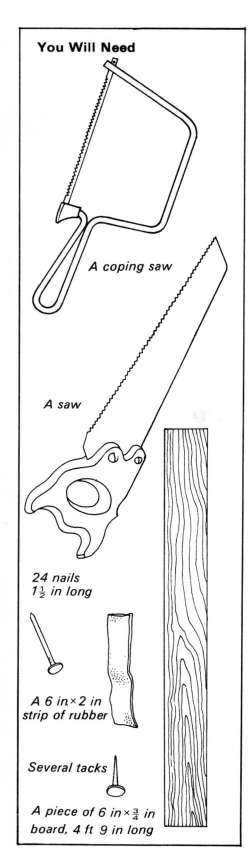

**You Will Need**

A coping saw

A saw

24 nails 1½ in long

A 6 in × 2 in strip of rubber

Several tacks

A piece of 6 in × ¾ in board, 4 ft 9 in long

This is a nest box which you can make. Blue tits or great tits may come to it. You will be able to watch the birds.

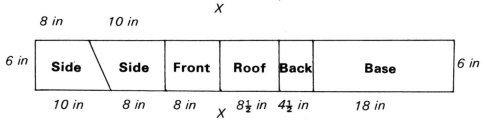

| | 8 in | 10 in | | X | | | |
|---|---|---|---|---|---|---|---|
| 6 in | Side | Side | Front | Roof | Back | Base | 6 in |
| | 10 in | 8 in | 8 in | 8½ in | 4½ in | 18 in | |

X

**Fig. 1**

You will need a large piece of wood which measures 6 in by 4 ft 9 in.

You need a sloping cut on the line XX.

54

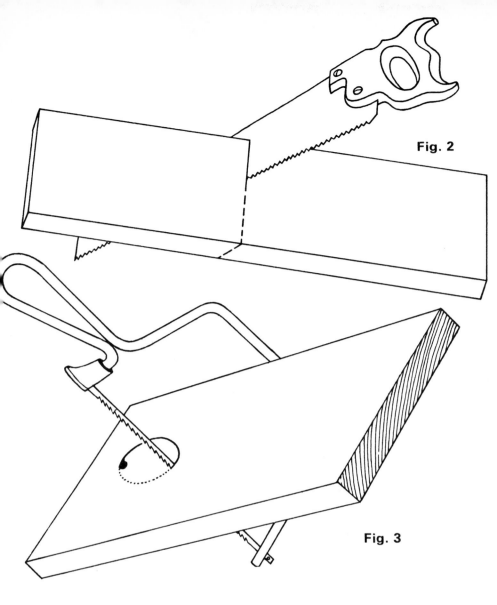

Fig. 2

Draw a circle
round a 10p piece.
Use a drill or
a coping saw
to make the hole. (Fig. 3)

4. Begin with the back.

5. Nail one side to
the back.
Nail it about half way
along the back.
Leave spaces at the
top and bottom
of the back.

6. Nail the base
on to the side and
the back.

7. Nail the second side
on to the base
and the back.

8. Nail on the front. (Fig. 4)

9. Tack one side of
the strip of rubber
to one side of the roof.

Fig. 3

10. Tack the other
side of the rubber
to the back of the
box. This makes
a hinge for the lid.

Treat the nest box
with wood preservative
to make it last longer.
Treat it only on the
outside of the box.

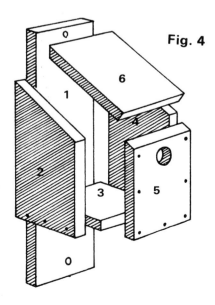

Fig. 4

1. Look at the plan
on page 54 to see how
to measure out the wood.

2. Cut the board
into lengths. (Fig. 1)
Make the slopes of
the two sides
by one diagonal cut. (Fig. 2)

3. To make the entrance
hole:
Measure one inch from
the top of the front.

# Making a Bird Table

## You Will Need

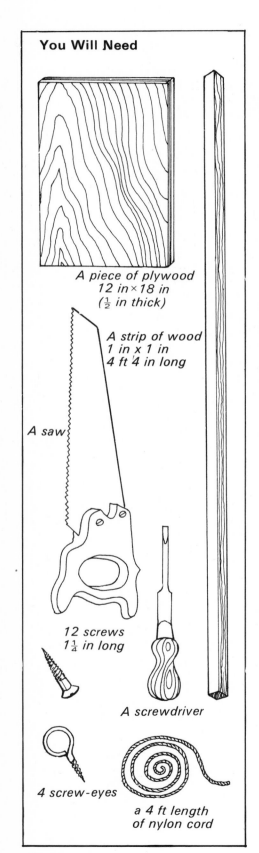

A piece of plywood
12 in × 18 in
($\frac{1}{2}$ in thick)

A strip of wood
1 in × 1 in
4 ft 4 in long

A saw

12 screws
1$\frac{1}{4}$ in long

A screwdriver

4 screw-eyes

a 4 ft length
of nylon cord

## Making the table

You will need all the things in the picture. Make sure you use the kind of plywood which can be used outside. Weak plywood will break up in the rain and snow.

## Food

Birds like to eat these things: Brown bread, cake, potatoes, bacon rind, apple cores, peanuts, coconuts, suet, different sorts of berries and seed mixtures.

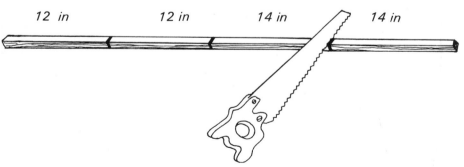

12 in    12 in    14 in    14 in

Cut the 1 in × 1 in piece of wood into two 12 in lengths and two 14 in lengths. Fix these to the edges of the plywood. The longer pieces go on the longer sides. The shorter pieces go on the shorter sides. The gaps in the edge are there so that water can drain off.

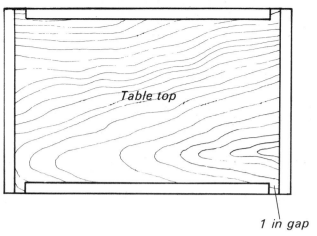

Table top

1 in gap

This picture shows where
to screw the strips
of wood. Make pencil marks
on the wood to help you.

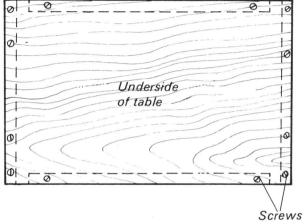

Underside
of table

Screws

This is the underneath of
the bird table. You can see
where to put the screws.
Drill holes for the screws.

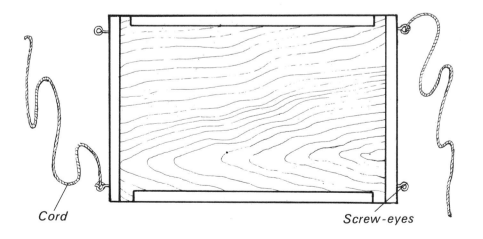

Cord

Screw-eyes

It is best to hang the bird
table on a branch or post.
You will need to put
in small screw-eyes at each

corner of the bird table.
Tie a piece of nylon cord
to each screw-eye.

## To make a Post Support

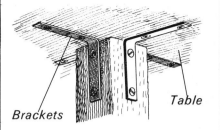

Brackets

Table

You need a piece
of 2 in × 2 in wood,
five ft high for a post.
1. Fix the post into the ground.
2. Screw four metal angle
brackets to the table and post.

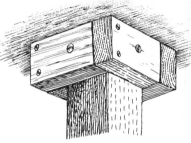

If you do not use brackets
you can make a square
using four short lengths of
2 in × 1 in wood.

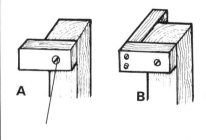

A

B

C

D

To make the square, screw the
first piece of 2 in × 1 in
wood to the post (A).
Screw the second piece of
wood to the first, as in B.
Do the same for the third
and fourth pieces as shown
in C and D. Screw the table
to the square.

# How to Draw Birds

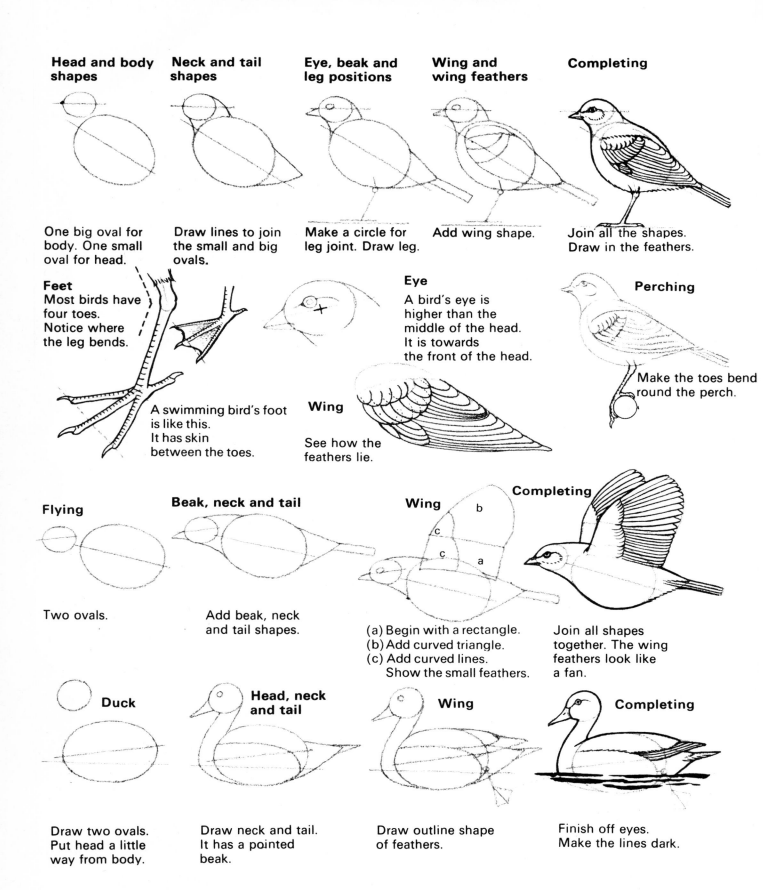

### Head and body shapes
One big oval for body. One small oval for head.

### Neck and tail shapes
Draw lines to join the small and big ovals.

### Eye, beak and leg positions
Make a circle for leg joint. Draw leg.

### Wing and wing feathers
Add wing shape.

### Completing
Join all the shapes. Draw in the feathers.

### Feet
Most birds have four toes. Notice where the leg bends.

A swimming bird's foot is like this. It has skin between the toes.

### Eye
A bird's eye is higher than the middle of the head. It is towards the front of the head.

### Wing
See how the feathers lie.

### Perching
Make the toes bend round the perch.

### Flying
Two ovals.

### Beak, neck and tail
Add beak, neck and tail shapes.

### Wing
(a) Begin with a rectangle.
(b) Add curved triangle.
(c) Add curved lines. Show the small feathers.

### Completing
Join all shapes together. The wing feathers look like a fan.

### Duck
Draw two ovals. Put head a little way from body.

### Head, neck and tail
Draw neck and tail. It has a pointed beak.

### Wing
Draw outline shape of feathers.

### Completing
Finish off eyes. Make the lines dark.

# Index

The numbers in **bold** type show where the the pictures are.